Last Airlift: A Vietnamese
Orphan's Rescue from War

Marsha Forchuk Skrypuch

Last Airlift

A Vietnamese Orphan's Rescue from War

pajamapress

First published in the United States in 2012
Text copyright © 2011 Marsha Skrypuch
This edition copyright © 2011 Pajama Press Inc.
10 9 8 7 6 5 4 3 2 1

The publisher has made every reasonable effort to trace the persons depicted in photographs as
well as the owners of copyrighted material. Any errors or omissions drawn to our attention
will be gladly rectified in future editions.

The publisher gratefully acknowledges the support of the Canada Council for the Arts and the
Ontario Arts Council for its publishing program. We acknowledge the financial support of the
Government of Canada through the Canada Book Fund (CBF) for our publishing activities.

 Canada Council   Conseil des Arts   ONTARIO ARTS COUNCIL
for the Arts   du Canada   CONSEIL DES ARTS DE L'ONTARIO

Library and Archives Canada Cataloguing in Publication

Skrypuch, Marsha Forchuk, 1954-
    Last airlift : a Vietnamese orphan's rescue from war / Marsha
Forchuk Skrypuch.

ISBN 978-0-9869495-4-8 (bound)

    1. Son Thi Anh, Tuyet--Juvenile literature. 2. Orphans--Vietnam--Ho Chi Minh
City--Biography--Juvenile literature. 3. Orphanages--Vietnam--Ho Chi Minh City--
Juvenile literature. 4. Vietnam War, 1961-1975--Children--Biography--Juvenile literature.
5. Airlift, Military--Vietnam--History--20th century--Juvenile literature. 6. Vietnam War,
1961-1975--Participation, Canadian--Juvenile literature. 7. Adopted children--Canada--
Biography--Juvenile literature. 8. Vietnamese Canadians--Biography--Juvenile literature.
I. Title.

DS559.8.C53S57 2011   j959.704'3086914092
C2011-905422-1

U.S. Publisher Cataloging-in-Publication Data (U.S.)

Forchuk Skrypuch, Marsha, 1954-
    Last airlift : a Vietnamese orphan's rescue from war / Marsha Forchuk Skrypuch.
[   ] p. : photos. ; cm.
Includes index.
Summary: The story of the last Canadian airlift rescue operation that left Saigon and
arrived in Toronto on April 13, 1975. Son Thi Anh Tuyet was one of the 57 babies
and children on that flight. Based on personal interviews and enhanced with archival
photographs, Tuyet's story of the Saigon orphanage and her flight to Canada is an
emotional and suspenseful journey.
ISBN-13: 978-0-9869495-4-8

1. Son Thi Anh, Tuyet – Juvenile literature. 2. Orphans – Vietnam – Ho Chi Minh City – Biography – Juvenile literature. 3. Vietnam War, 1961-1975 – Children – Biography – Juvenile literature. 4. Airlift, Military – Vietnam--History – 20th century – Juvenile literature. 5. Vietnamese Canadians – Biography – Juvenile literature. I. Title.
959.70431 dc23   DS559.8 C53S66 2012

Cover and book design–Rebecca Buchanan

Manufactured by Webcom. Printed in Canada.

Pajama Press Inc.
469 Richmond St E, Toronto Ontario, Canada
www.pajamapress.ca

Photo Credits

Cover: Rice terrace–Shutterstock/©Pattarawat Teparagul; Hercules 130, Major Cliff Zacharias–courtesy of Major (Retired) Cliff Zacharias; Tuyet arriving in Canada–Doug Griffin/Toronto Star; Tuyet passport photograph–courtesy of Dorothy Morris; 1-1: Birth certificate–courtesy of Dorothy Morris; 1-2: helicopters–Getty Images/Archive Holdings Inc.; 2-1: tanks in Saigon–© Jacques Pavlovsky/Sygma/CORBIS; 2-2: civilians flee–© Jacques Pavlovsky/Sygma/CORBIS; 2-3: Hercules 130–courtesy of Major (Retired) Cliff Zacharias; 3-1: boxed babies–courtesy of 426 Squadron, 8 Wing/Canadian Forces Base Trenton; 3-2: Major Cliff Zacharias–courtesy of Major (Retired) Cliff Zacharias; 4-1: aid workers assist children; 4-2: children on rescue flight; 4-3: aid workers in Hong Kong–426 Squadron, 8 Wing/Canadian Forces Base Trenton; 4-4: Tuyet arriving in Canada; 5-1: orphan with care worker; 5-2: medical staff examines baby; 5-3: toddler with new bear–Doug Griffin/Toronto Star/GetStock; 6-1: Adoption Order form–courtesy of Dorothy Morris; 6-2: Morris Family; 7-1: newspaper headline–*Brantford Expositor*; 8-1: Tuyet's passport photos; 9-1: Tuyet's Vietnamese handwriting; 10-1: Tuyet with Linh, 1975; 10-2: Tuyet and siblings–courtesy of Dorothy Morris; 11-1: Canadian Forces Base Trenton–courtesy of Major (Retired) Cliff Zacharias; 11-2: Corporal with 2 orphans–courtesty of 426 Squadron, 8 Wing/Canadian Forces Base Trenton; 11-3: Marsha and Tuyet–Brian Thompson

With admiration,
to Dorothy Morris
and the late John Morris

Table of Contents

TÒA HÀNH-CHÁNH QUẬN NHÌ

Số hiệu : 654̶6̶3̶

*

VIỆT-NAM CỘNG-HÒA

HỘ·TỊCH

TRÍCH-LỤC BỘ KHAI SANH

Năm một ngàn chín trăm ꞏꞏꞏ muoi ꞏꞏꞏ (19ꞏꞏ)

Tên, họ đứa nhỏ	NGU-THI ANH-TUYET
Phái	Nu
Ngày sanh	mồ thang tam nam mot ngan chin tram sau muoi sau - 11giờ30
Nơi sanh	Saigon, 204 Cong-Quỳnh
Tên, họ người Cha	///
Tuổi	///
Nghề-nghiệp	///
Nơi cư-ngụ	///
Tên, họ người mẹ	NGU-THI-KL
Tuổi	hai muoi chin
Nghề-nghiệp	Noi tro
Nơi cư-ngụ	Saigon, 68 Yen-Đo
Vợ chánh hay thứ	///

MIỄN LỆ-PHÍ
HỒ-SƠ HÀNH-CHÁNH

Saigon, ngày 2̶ tháng 5 năm 19ꞏꞏ

TRÍCH-LỤC Y BỔN CHÁNH :

Saigon, ngày 25 tháng 8 năm 197̶7̶

QUẬN-TRƯỞNG QUẬN NHÌ

TRƯƠNG HỮU XƯƠNG

1-1   *Tuyet's birth certificate*

Chapter One

Early April 1975

Tuyet could not remember a time before the orphanage.

She thought that all children lived together in a building with sleeping rooms, a play area, school, and chapel. She remembered sleeping together with the older girls on a wood-slat floor, without blankets or pillows. She would wake up each morning with marks from the wood slats on her cheek.

Tuyet would clean her teeth using her finger and salt. Day and night she wore a pajama-like cotton top and drawstring pants. The nuns would give each child a newly laundered set of clothing every three days or so.

In the morning, she would line up with the other girls. One of the nuns would rip bread from a giant loaf and give a piece to each child. Her meals consisted of fish, rice, plain water. There weren't enough chopsticks to go around, so they used their hands.

The orphanage included boys and younger children—and lots of babies. At the age of eight, Tuyet was one of the oldest. She was expected to help out with the younger ones without being asked. It was her duty, but she didn't mind.

Tuyet would see the older boys in class, when they played together in the indoor courtyard, and at chapel three times a day. The priest who said Mass was the only man she saw in the building, except for the soldiers.

1-2 *Many helicopters were used in the Vietnam war*

The children stayed inside at all times; it was not safe outside. Tuyet could not remember ever seeing the sky above her head.

When she heard the *whop-whop-whop* of helicopters, Tuyet would hide. She couldn't remember exactly what it was that she was afraid of, but when she put her fingers to her scalp, she could feel dents. She had a large burn scar on her back and another long scar under her chin. She couldn't remember when the injuries happened, but it must have been before the orphanage.

Tuyet remembered the big door opening and American soldiers coming in with stuffed toys, spinning tops, and hard candy. The other children would crowd around the men, competing for attention and gifts. But Tuyet would hide. She wasn't afraid of the Americans, but she had polio. Her left ankle was so weak that she walked on her heel. In order to move forward, she had to push her left knee with her left hand. She had calluses on her knee, because she pushed it so often. She was afraid that if the soldiers saw her foot and weak leg, they would take her to the hospital. And then the doctors would cut her foot open to try to fix it.

Sometimes she played with the other children—

simple games with elastics and chopsticks. The children also made a long skipping rope by joining together many elastics. With her weak foot, there was no way Tuyet would ever be able to join in such a game. She could only sit and watch as the others skipped rope.

Some of the children were mean to Tuyet. One boy would crush lit cigarettes on her leg. But there was another boy who was friendly. They would play together as often as they could.

Before school started, Tuyet and the girls would line up. The boys would line up, too. There were even some children from outside the orphanage who came to their school.

Tuyet would sit at her desk, fascinated by the inkwell and fountain pen. She would draw patterns with the ink on paper. Like the other children, Tuyet also had chalk and a slate. She could draw or write something with the chalk, then make it disappear by rubbing it with her hand or a piece of cloth. She vividly remembered using the Vietnamese alphabet, although she couldn't remember what else she learned. When she did well in her lessons, the teacher would paste a small gold star onto her work.

In another room, Tuyet and the other children would gather around the nun who sat in a chair. They would sit on the floor and memorize Bible verses.

The nuns were not always kind. Once, during naptime, Tuyet's eyes were still open as she played with a lock of her hair. A nun came by and told Tuyet to close her eyes and sleep. Then the nun hit her on the fingers, hard, with a bamboo stick.

The nuns would play the piano and they would sing. Tuyet loved that. She remembered one particular night they called "Christmas Eve." She didn't understand what Christmas was, but the nuns gave each child a bowl of special soup instead of their usual meal. The children were allowed to stay up late. The nuns set up a screen and showed them an American movie. It was in English and the children didn't understand the words. But in one scene, a white man and woman kissed each other, and Tuyet and the others giggled in embarrassment.

Another year on that special night, each child was given an orange.

Today, there isn't much more that Tuyet can remember about the orphanage before her life changed forever.

And although she cannot remember where she came from, Tuyet does recall two visitors from outside.

"A woman would come to see me. She would bring a young boy. I would sit on her lap for a while and then they would leave. Maybe that was my mother. Maybe the boy was my brother.

"After a while, they stopped coming."

Chapter Two

When Things Changed
April 11, 1975

Tuyet didn't know about the world beyond her building. But she could hear the soldiers, helicopters, gunfire, and explosions. She had always lived with those sounds in the background.

On the day her life changed, the doors of the orphanage were opened, but instead of soldiers with candy, the children saw a white Volkswagen van screeching to a halt. A man jumped out. He wasn't a soldier or a priest, and he didn't look Vietnamese. He called out to the nuns in a language Tuyet did not understand. Beyond the van, the streets were full of people running. Many carried suitcases; others carried children. Some of the people were weeping while others were screaming.

The man helped the nuns rush around, packing

diapers, formula, water, and bedding. Everything was placed by the door. Tuyet and the older children stared in confusion as the adults gathered boxes and lined them up at the entrance. The nuns carried the babies from their sleeping area and bundled them in blankets. Then each baby was placed in a box. Some boxes were big enough for two babies.

The man had a handful of plastic straps. He read aloud the name printed on each strap, and then a nun would find the right baby and attach the strap to the baby's wrist.

2-1

North Vietnamese tanks enter Saigon

"Son Thi Anh Tuyet," said the man.

Tuyet looked up in surprise. Why was he calling her name? She wasn't a baby. One of the nuns walked up to her. "Let me have your arm," she said. "You'll be going, too."

Tuyet rubbed the snug plastic wristband as the adults loaded the boxes of babies into the back of the van. Suddenly, the man lifted Tuyet into his arms and carried her to the van. Tuyet looked back over his shoulder at the other children—the girls she had slept with for as long as she could remember, that one special boy who had played with her. They all stood huddled together, round-eyed with fear. Was it better to go or stay behind?

As the man set her down on the floor of the van, Tuyet's special friend rushed forward and thrust a small package into her hand.

The back of the van was hot and stuffy, and it was packed so tightly with the boxes of babies that the corner of one box jabbed painfully into Tuyet's hip. But she sat obediently where she had been put. Her left foot and leg hurt most of the time anyway, and she had learned to suffer in silence.

The man climbed into the driver's seat. Tuyet leaned over to get a view of the passenger seat. A frail newborn had been strapped carefully in place beside him.

The van jerked forward. Tuyet turned to stare out the back window as the van slowly pulled away from the orphanage and into the road thick with people and cars. She waved goodbye to her special friend, the nuns, and the other children. She tried to watch them for as long as she could, but the van rounded a corner and the nuns and children disappeared.

Tuyet looked down at the small package she held in her hand, and opened it. Inside was a rosary—a necklace to use for counting prayers—made with pale coral and crystal beads. It sparkled like the gold stars the nuns would award for good work. Tuyet could feel the tears well up in her eyes. Would she ever see that boy again? She let the cool beads slip through her fingers and, for a moment, she thought of nothing but the boy's face. She would try to remember him always. She slipped the shiny beads back into their package and tucked it deep into the pocket of her pants.

Tuyet was jolted out of her thoughts when the van lurched sideways. She gazed out the window at the tangle of traffic and frantic people. In the distance, flames licked up the sides of buildings and smoke billowed high above. Although the sound of gunfire was everywhere, Tuyet felt safe in the van. But she was hot and her hip was sore. She shifted her position so the box wouldn't jab into her so much.

2-2

South Vietnamese civilians flee as Saigon falls to North Vietnamese forces

Some of the babies began to wail. The toddlers squirmed and tried to get out of the boxes, but they were packed in so tightly that there was no place to squirm to. The driver was concentrating on the road; there was no one but Tuyet to help the children and babies. She tried to calm them by singing softly and caressing the tear-streaked cheeks closest to her. But they were as hot as she felt. Probably they were as thirsty as she was, too.

Tuyet looked back out the window and marveled at the variety of people in the street. Most of the women in the orphanage had been nuns, with their starched white habits and clinking beads. The priest was always in robes and the other men were in their American uniforms. But here, the Vietnamese men wore white shirts and dark pants. The women were in long baggy trousers and pastel-colored tops, and their lush black hair hung down their backs. Some wore conical bamboo hats. Wherever they were going, the way was clogged with others going in the same direction.

It seemed like hours, but finally the driver sighed with relief and said something Tuyet couldn't understand. He pointed out the front window.

In front of them stood tall fences topped with barbed wire. People crowded around, trying to push their way through the gate. Viet Cong soldiers pushed back with their guns. Many of the people reached for the tall wire. One man threw his suitcase all the way over the fence.

He clutched onto the wire and pulled himself up. He was almost at the top when a soldier caught him and dragged him down. All of the people appeared frantic to get to the other side.

The van pulled up to a locked gate. Soldiers held back the crowd and the van inched forward. The driver rolled down his window and showed a piece of paper to one of the soldiers. That soldier pushed through the crowd and unlocked the gate, sliding it back just far enough for the van to drive through. The van swayed as people jumped on top of it. Some pounded on the window, and Tuyet hid her face in her hands. Finally, the van was on the other side of the gate. Tuyet looked back to see a soldier pull the fence closed again as another held back the crowd.

Without all the people, it seemed suddenly still. The noise from the outside was gone, making Tuyet more aware of the babies and toddlers in the boxes.

"It's all right," Tuyet said in a cooing voice, hoping to comfort the hot and frightened infants. But she had no idea if it *was* all right.

The van drove across a wide empty space and pulled up in front of a strange winged building with a huge door that yawned wide. Many foreign-looking adults scurried about, some carrying toddlers or boxes of babies, others standing by, hands on hips.

2-3   *Hercules C-130 aircraft*

Their uniforms made the American soldiers look alike. But Tuyet had noticed before how different their skin looked. Some were pale pink or almost white; others were brown and black. Few were golden like her. And they were always men.

The foreign adults were mostly female. They had pale skin splotched with pink and pale wispy hair in different hues—yellow, orange, brown, and white. Instead of uniforms, they wore complicated clothing, like flowered skirts and pastel dresses with straps, buckles, and ribbons. But their faces still looked the same to Tuyet.

The back door opened and a whoosh of fresher air enveloped her. A man who wasn't a soldier reached in and grabbed one of the boxes that held two tiny babies. Holding the box with care, he rushed to the ramp that led into the winged building. A woman came forward, and then another, and another. As each wrapped her arms around a box, Tuyet pushed the remaining boxes forward so they would be easier to reach. Soon, all the babies were out of the van and Tuyet was left sitting by herself. She wondered if she had been put in the van just to help with the boxes. Would she be going back to her old home now? Back to her special friend?

Other vans and cars pulled up. Workers ran up to those vans and quickly unloaded the children and babies with efficiency. Some older children hopped out, and Tuyet strained to see them more clearly.

But she recognized no one.

A cloud of orange hair poked into the back of Tuyet's van. A hand fluttered to hold the hair in place briefly. Tuyet stared into startling blue eyes and a pink face damp with sweat.

"It's your turn, now," the woman said in Vietnamese. Tuyet scrambled toward the woman, who held out her arms to carry her. But Tuyet shook her head.

"I will walk," she said.

Chapter Three
The Airplane

"What is that place?" asked Tuyet, pointing at the strange winged building.

"A giant airplane called a Hercules," said the woman in Vietnamese. "It will go up into the sky and take us away from the war. It will take you to safety."

Tuyet was amazed. The strange winged building was an airplane! She knew the sound of airplanes. She had heard their roar almost as often as she'd heard the *wop-wop-wop* of helicopters. But this airplane was bigger than her orphanage. She never imagined that an airplane could be so big.

Tuyet sat with her legs poised over the edge of the van door. Gingerly, she slid down, the heel of her weak foot landing painfully on the oven-hot tarmac. She hopped beside the woman to show she could move quickly, but her feet felt like they were burning up.

"Let me carry you," said the woman. "The pavement is too hot for bare feet."

When she was lifted up, Tuyet had a view of the entire airport and beyond. The airplane she was being taken to wasn't the only one preparing to leave. She could see two others and lots of activity. Above her, the sky was black with spirals of smoke. Where was the black smoke coming from?

Tuyet scanned the lush green expanse of rice paddies beyond the airport runways. And then she saw it: the crashed remains of an airplane with smoke billowing out of it.

She pointed. "That airplane didn't stay up in the air."

The woman's eyes filled with tears. "Don't worry," she said. "We will be safe."

But how could Tuyet not worry?

The entry to the airplane was like a big angled ramp the width of a room. Tuyet clung to the woman's shoulders as she was carried in. The woman set her down on the floor in the cargo hold amidst boxes of babies, canvas bags, straps, and crates of formula, food, and medicine.

The woman began to push the boxes of babies close

together. In order to make sure the boxes wouldn't slide around, she secured them with a long, sticky strap that looped over several boxes at once.

Tuyet saw that it was time to make herself useful. Without being asked, she copied what the woman was doing and strapped in a second row of screaming and wriggling babies.

Soon more people brought box after box through the wide door. Everyone scurried about, finding places for the babies and taping them in.

3-1   *Boxed babies strapped in place and ready for takeoff*

The giant door closed and the inside of the airplane quickly became hot and stuffy. Worse than the heat was the smell of dirty diapers. Tuyet was used to heat and babies' diapers, but she had never felt so closed in. Her heart pounded. Sweat trickled down her back, getting her shirt all wet. Her hair stuck to her forehead and neck.

The baby boxes covered the floor area of the cargo hold. On the upper level, a row of seats ran along the sides of the aircraft, close to the windows. A set of metal stairs connected the two levels.

Tuyet reached her hand out and caressed the baby closest to her, but as she cooed a lullaby into the baby's ear, she heard a huge roaring sound. Her body trembled with terror. Was this airplane about to go up in flames like the one she had seen in the rice paddy?

Tuyet felt a hand on her arm. She looked up. It was one of the women who spoke her language.

"That's just one of the engines," the woman explained. "The pilot turned it on to cool the air. There are three more engines, so don't be frightened when they start up."

Tuyet nodded. Maybe it would be fine.

Just then, a small door at the front of the airplane was

pulled open from the outside. Four Viet Cong soldiers stepped in, armed with machine guns. They looked angry.

The woman appeared frightened, but she stood and walked up to the soldiers. "Everything is in order," she said.

"We need to see their papers," said one of the soldiers, pointing his machine gun at the babies and children.

The woman hurried to the cockpit and came back with a stack of forms. She handed them to one of the soldiers. He examined each form carefully, matching them up with the wrist straps as he did so. A baby not far from Tuyet had no wrist strap.

"You have no papers for her," he said. "And no papers for that one," he added, pointing to an older toddler who was trying to stand up in his box.

The woman's face stayed calm and strong, but her lips were a pale thin line. "Just a minute." She headed back to the cockpit.

For a minute, nothing happened.

Then, suddenly, one of the pilots burst out of the cockpit. He wore a fancy hat with gold braid, and his face was purple with rage. He hollered something in another language at the two soldiers.

The sight of the raging pilot terrified Tuyet, but it also startled the soldiers. They backed out of the door and ran down the steps. The pilot pulled the door shut with all his might and locked it from the inside, sighing with relief. He took off the hat with the fancy braid.

All at once, Tuyet understood. The pilot had tricked the soldiers into thinking he was an important commander who had to be obeyed. It made her smile.

The pilot went back into the cockpit and the woman stepped out again. She looked almost happy.

"You need to get into a seat," said a different woman, who crouched down in front of Tuyet. "Can you walk, or do you want me to carry you?"

Tuyet was afraid that she might lose her balance and hurt the babies if she tried to cross the middle of the cargo hold without help. The babies and extra supplies were so closely packed together. Tuyet reached out her arms and the woman picked her up. She held Tuyet above the babies and helped her to the steps and into a seat by the window, not far from the cockpit.

"I will strap you in," the woman said kindly.

For a moment, Tuyet's heart thumped with panic. She did not want to be tied down. "Can I get out if I need to?"

"Of course you can. Watch." The woman flicked the metal clamp with her finger and the seatbelt popped open. Tuyet tried opening and closing the seatbelt herself a few times. She began to relax.

"But you must be strapped in when the airplane takes off," the woman added, then she straightened up and walked down the aisle.

At that moment, even though Tuyet was in an airplane jam-packed with babies and children—along with the adults who were working to save them—she felt utterly alone. She remembered the rosary her special friend had given her. Holding it would make her feel better. She reached into her pocket. But her pocket was empty.

The package was gone.

The rosary must have dropped out in the van, or maybe later, when she was helping with the babies. Tears filled her eyes and spilled down her cheeks. She tried to breathe slowly, to make the tears go away. She didn't want anyone to see that she was crying, so she closed her eyes.

Her hands felt something soft. She opened her eyes. A cloth doll. She looked up. One of the women, smiling, hovered over her. Tuyet hugged the doll to her chest.

"Thank you," she said, looking into the woman's gold-colored eyes.

The woman patted Tuyet's hand. "It's going to be fine."

Tuyet had never owned a doll before. The visiting soldiers sometimes brought dolls to a few of the children in the orphanage, but never to Tuyet. She held the doll up to her face and breathed in its fresh newness. For just a few moments, she was able to forget losing her friend, losing the life she had known. Maybe everything would be all right.

Tuyet looked out the window. From where she sat, she had a clear view of the smoking plane in the distance. She closed her eyes and clasped the doll to her chest.

The plane moved forward. Tuyet exhaled in relief. Soon they would be away from here. She didn't know if she was looking forward to the future, but at least the uncertainty would soon be over.

The Hercules shuddered to a stop.

Tuyet opened her eyes and looked out the window. Two people stood on the runway, in front of the airplane! Didn't they realize they might have been run over? How had they got past the soldiers and the fence?

Tuyet squinted to get a better look. The man wore

the distinctive collar of a priest. He was holding tight to the hand of a girl who looked about the same age as Tuyet.

The pilot called out, "You've got to get out of the way!"

"You must take this girl with you!" the priest hollered back.

3-2

Major Cliff Zacharias

"We're not allowed to," shouted the pilot.

"Then we'll stand here in front of the plane."

The cockpit door opened. The pilot stomped out,

looking angry and frustrated. He unlatched the door at the front of the airplane and pushed it open. Moments later, the girl's head appeared in the doorway.

Tuyet looked out the window, where the priest now stood alone. He bowed in thanks and walked off the runway.

The pilot led the girl to an empty seat in front of Tuyet and quickly strapped her in. Then he headed back to the cockpit.

The girl wept quietly. Tuyet leaned forward and said, "It will be okay."

The second engine began to roar, then the third and, at last, the fourth.

"Get ready for takeoff," called the pilot through the speaker system.

Tuyet leaned back into the seat and clutched her doll. Under her breath, she whispered, "Please let this plane fly, please let this plane fly."

The Hercules moved again. From where Tuyet sat, she could see one of the giant wings. Suddenly, part of the wing folded down. Oh no! Was this how the other plane had crashed? Tuyet whimpered.

"It's the wing flaps," said the woman in the seat

behind her. "They're supposed to do that."

Tuyet closed her eyes and repeated her wish, "Please let this airplane fly!"

Just as the wish left her lips, the Hercules lifted. It angled up to the sky so sharply that Tuyet could feel blood rushing to her head and the skin on her face pulling tight. The babies, who had been whimpering half-heartedly, began to scream. The airplane went higher. Babies cried louder. Tuyet felt like the plane was going straight up into the air. Her ears popped. She was afraid to breathe.

The plane leveled out. The babies stopped screaming and suddenly it was silent. Then the woman behind her said, loud enough for everyone to hear, "We're safe now."

Tuyet felt tears of relief rise in her throat. They were safe!

But she was still afraid.

Chapter Four

Linh

Once the plane was in the air, the adults unbuckled their seatbelts and went down the metal steps to get to the babies. Tuyet opened the buckle to her own seatbelt. It felt good to have it off. She leaned forward to speak to the sobbing girl.

"My name is Tuyet," she said. "I am happy to meet you."

It took the girl a moment to compose herself enough to answer. "My name is Linh*," she said hesitantly. "I am happy to meet you as well, Tuyet."

"We should help with the babies," said Tuyet. "I can smell a lot of dirty diapers."

That made Linh smile. "Good idea."

Tuyet gingerly got out of her seat and made her way

* Not her real name, which has been changed to protect her privacy.

down the steps. Linh was not far behind. When Tuyet looked back, she saw Linh glance at her weak leg.

"Do you need help?" asked Linh.

"I can manage on my own," said Tuyet. She hated it when people assumed she couldn't do things because of her foot.

4-1   *Aid workers assist the children during the flight*

Once she was in the lower part of the Hercules, Tuyet crawled on her hands and knees between the crying babies. It was so crowded with boxes and supplies that Tuyet did not want to risk losing her balance. The women didn't have to tell her what to do. She changed diapers when she found them wet, and she gave bottles of water to babies who felt hot.

Linh stood by awkwardly, staring at the organized chaos all around her. She didn't seem to know what to do.

"Take this baby," said Tuyet, reaching into one of the boxes and thrusting a screaming baby into Linh's arms. "She probably has gas. Hold her up to your shoulder and pat her on the back. Walk around. The movement will help."

Linh followed instructions while Tuyet continued looking after the babies. Some time later, Linh came back, a sleeping baby in her arms. Tuyet gently took the baby from her and set him in his box.

"How do you know what to do with babies?" Linh asked.

Tuyet met her eyes. "I've been looking after babies for as long as I can remember."

Linh continued to take directions from Tuyet and, between the two of them, they settled many babies. Being busy helped Tuyet relax. And with the company of Linh, Tuyet didn't feel quite so alone.

As they worked, they overheard some of the women speak to each other in a language that they couldn't understand.

"They're speaking English," Linh told Tuyet. "Be careful how you answer when people say things to you in English."

"I don't know any English," said Tuyet. "How could I possibly answer?"

"Whenever someone asks you something in English, answer, *No*," said Linh. "That will stop them from doing what they were going to do."

Tuyet practiced the English word under her breath. It was hard to believe that one simple word could be the answer to everything in English, but she was grateful for Linh's advice.

The great Hercules airplane landed in Hong Kong. Tuyet, Linh, and the others were taken to a hospital.

A man, who was dressed in white with a mask over his face, shone a light into Tuyet's ears.

"Good," he said in Vietnamese.

He listened to her heart and had her breathe in and out. He also examined her weak foot and leg, and that worried Tuyet. But he wrote something on his clipboard, and his eyes crinkled into a smile.

Tuyet

4-2   *Tuyet and other children inside the Hercules during the flight. Captain Dessureault of 426 Squadron is in the foreground, holding one of the children.*

"You are healthy enough."

Linh was examined next and she got the same good news.

Tuyet, Linh, and the babies and children declared healthy enough to travel were taken to a section of the Hong Kong hospital where they could rest and recover. For the next few days, they were bathed, dressed in clean clothing, and fed lots of good food.

The orphans who were too sick to travel were taken to a different part of the hospital for treatment.

After their few days' rest, Tuyet, Linh, and the other healthy orphans boarded a Canadian Pacific flight. The boxes of babies, care workers, and children took up a good part of the airplane, but there were regular passengers on it, too. Many pitched in to help feed babies, change their diapers, and rock them to sleep.

There were more flights between Hong Kong and Toronto, but they all blended into one long dream. It felt as if time had stopped. Vaguely, Tuyet remembered singing songs with Linh and trying to get babies to laugh. She remembered feeding the older toddlers a rice and

4-3   *Aid workers helping some orphans in Hong Kong*

broth mixture, and that's what she and Linh also ate. That, and plenty of bananas.

The airplane landed in Vancouver and they changed planes one last time. This time, it was an Air Canada commercial flight.

A few hours later, they arrived at the Toronto airport.

A care worker pinned on Tuyet's shirt a piece of paper with the number 23 on it. Then the children and babies were taken off the airplane in numerical order.

The first thing Tuyet noticed when she approached the open door was cold air blowing on her face. Someone quickly draped a white blanket around her shoulders and she clasped it around herself for warmth. It was always hot and humid in Saigon; Tuyet had never felt air like this before. She gulped the breeze into her lungs as if it were a cool, soothing drink.

She sniffed the air, and the scent brought back a distant memory of freshly ploughed earth. No smell of smoke.

No sound of war.

Then Tuyet looked up into the sky, and she gasped. It was like a soft blanket of black, but she could see points of sparkling white light. Had the war followed her here?

She pointed up and asked a care worker who stood by her side, "Are those bombs?"

"No," said the man. "Those are stars. They are beautiful to look at and they will not harm you."

Stars. Tuyet remembered the bits of foil her teacher would stick onto her schoolwork when she did well. Those were called stars, too. She looked back up at the sparkling points of light. Stars were *real*? The sight of so many of them in the sky made her feel proud. It was as if the sky was telling her that she had done a good job, helping all those babies through their long journey together.

Tuyet knew that she could walk down the steps from the airplane on her own. But she was so tired that she didn't protest when the care worker picked her up and carried her down.

Suddenly, a bright flash startled her.

And another.

Tuyet whimpered in fear. She buried her face in the care worker's neck.

"It's okay," said the man. "Those aren't guns. They are just cameras. These people are taking your picture for the newspapers."

Tuyet knew about flash cameras. Once, a soldier

had brought a flash camera to the orphanage. Tuyet had thought it was a new kind of weapon and she had stayed well hidden. Shortly before she was evacuated, a nun had taken her picture. But that camera was small and Tuyet trusted the nun.

4-4   *Tuyet arrives in Toronto*

Tuyet poked her head up and squinted, trying to get a good view of the cameras in the dark. The care worker was right. The cameras were much bigger than any she had seen before. But they were definitely not weapons.

Once everyone was off the airplane, they were all loaded onto a bus. Tuyet and Linh sat beside each other.

Tuyet said, "What is going to happen to us now?"

"I'm not sure," said Linh, gripping one of Tuyet's hands in her own. "But remember to say no if someone asks you something in English. It's the only way to stay safe."

Tuyet looked out the window as the bus pulled away from the airport. The crowds of people were still there, flashing away with their cameras. Tuyet didn't want to look at those people. She gazed up into the night sky, willing the stars to calm her and fill her with courage.

The bus jolted forward and Tuyet was reminded of the earlier van ride that had taken her away from everything familiar. Where would this bus take her? Once the rest of the children in the van had all been adopted, would the adults send her back to Saigon? Or would she go to work in an orphanage in this strange city? Would Linh work with her, or would her friend be adopted?

As the bus maneuvered through the quiet streets of

nighttime Toronto, Tuyet was struck by how different the city looked from Saigon. There were no people running through the streets with their suitcases, no soldiers with guns, no fires in the distance, no smoke. Just fresh, cold air and tall buildings that sparkled with multicolored lights. Some of the lights outlined pictures and others spelled out words. Some of the letters were the same as in the Vietnamese alphabet. Tuyet tried to sound the words out, but nothing made sense.

It wasn't long before the bus stopped. A pale brick building loomed out of the darkness.

"Maybe this is where we're going to live now," said Tuyet.

Linh didn't answer. Her eyes were wide with fear. They got off the bus. Linh gripped one of Tuyet's hands in her own, and the two girls slowly walked forward with the rest of the tired group.

5-1 *A care worker looks after a baby at Surrey Place*

Chapter Five
Surrey Place

The children were lined up by numbers once again. A man looked at the information on Tuyet's wrist band and wrote something onto a form. Next, someone with a camera took her picture, but this time it didn't flash. Tuyet watched with curiosity as a piece of paper came out of the camera. The man held it up to her and smiled. It was a picture of a sad-looking girl.

"That's you," said Linh.

Tuyet blinked in surprise. She had never seen a picture of herself before, and there were no mirrors in the orphanage. Did she really wear her sadness on her face for all to see?

Tuyet watched the man glue the picture onto the information form.

Next, she was taken to a room with rows of iron beds. Children, some of them crying, occupied the beds. More adults stood by, dressed in white.

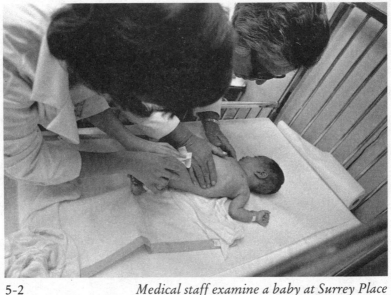

5-2   *Medical staff examine a baby at Surrey Place*

A man sat Tuyet on a bed, listened to her chest, and looked inside her mouth with a flashlight and a stick. He held her hair up and looked into her ears. Then he used a little hammer to tap her good knee. He looked at her weak knee and foot, but he was so gentle, it didn't hurt at all. He wrote something on her information sheet.

Next, he held her arm firmly and pressed a metal contraption on it. *Bang.* Tuyet jumped.

"All done," said the man in Vietnamese.

Tuyet looked down at the place on her arm where the metal contraption had been, and saw a circle of little pinpricks. It didn't hurt.

A man who was Vietnamese came to the room and took her by the hand. Tuyet had been so focused on what was happening to her that she had lost track of Linh. Now she looked frantically around the room.

"Do you know where Linh is?" she asked the man.

"Probably upstairs," the man answered. "Once you're finished with the medical examination, I'll take you up to join her."

The rest of her examination didn't take long. The man took Tuyet out of the room and into the hallway, where he stopped in front of two metal doors.

"This is an elevator," he said. "Quicker than stairs."

The doors opened and they both stepped inside a small room. The doors closed. Tuyet could feel panic rise in her stomach, but man was calm and the door opened quickly again. They stepped out into a big room, where metal beds and bassinettes were arranged in rows.

Linh sat on one bed, and she held a stuffed bear on her lap. "Tuyet!" she called. "Take this bed beside me."

On the bed next to Linh sat a colorful stuffed doll with a plaid skirt and button eyes.

"Is that for me?" asked Tuyet.

"Yes," the man answered and smiled down at her. "Each child gets a toy."

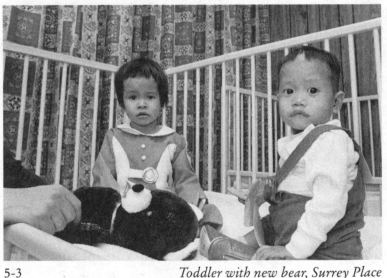

5-3   *Toddler with new bear, Surrey Place*

Tuyet reached for the doll. Then she remembered. Where was the doll she'd been given on the flight? It had felt so good to have something of her own. How could she have left it behind? Tuyet hugged the new doll to her chest. This one she would not forget.

Tuyet pulled herself up onto the bed beside Linh. The man brought each girl a glass of juice and a cookie. As Tuyet sat there, nibbling on the cookie and feeling the warmth of her friend by her side, she felt happy.

"This is not bad," she said with a grin.

"I am pretty sure we won't be staying here," said Linh. "I think we will be given to families."

Tuyet had heard about children getting new families. At the orphanage in Saigon, some of children were taken away. The nuns said they had gone to new families. But none of the children ever came back to tell the others what happened next. Did the new families feed them? Did they make them do chores? Tuyet didn't know. She looked around the room and took a deep breath. It could be worse. This place was clean and bright, and there were no sounds of war.

Tuyet thought about that woman and boy who visited her in the orphanage. Were they her family? She thought of the special boy at the orphanage. Was he her family, too?

She clutched her new doll and thought of the other doll and the rosary she had lost. Were families as replaceable as dolls and rosaries? Linh was now Tuyet's only friend. Tuyet felt tears welling up inside her. Would Linh be lost to her now, as well?

"Will you promise to stay with me always?" Tuyet asked Linh.

"It is not up to us," said Linh. "But I will try."

"If they try to take you away from me, you can just say *no*," said Tuyet.

Linh smiled. "Good idea."

With that, Linh finished the last of her juice and cookie. She curled up on the cot and, hugging her new stuffed bear, closed her eyes.

Tuyet walked over to her own bed and sat down. Linh was already deep in an exhausted slumber. Even Linh did not need Tuyet. She felt so alone.

The women in white carried more babies into the room. Tuyet longed to help. In the airplanes, it had felt so good to prove that she was useful.

The babies looked clean and well fed. But as soon as the women put them into their own bassinettes, the babies began to scream.

Tuyet felt like screaming, too. The babies must be exhausted. Why were they crying?

As she stared at the babies, Tuyet suddenly realized the problem. When the babies were put to bed at the orphanage, they were always close enough to touch. Here, the babies were separated from each other. They weren't used to being alone.

Tuyet stood up. She scanned the room to see if the man who spoke Vietnamese was still there, but he had left. She went up to one of the workers, a woman with yellow hair held in place with a pink elastic band.

Tuyet tapped the woman's arm. "The babies," she said. "They want to be close to each other."

The woman stared back at Tuyet, her face blank. She didn't understand Vietnamese.

Tuyet went up to Linh and shook her shoulder. Linh sat up, rubbing the sleep from her eyes.

"The babies are upset," said Tuyet. "They're too far apart."

Linh gave a huge yawn and stood up. "I guess we'll have to show them."

Tuyet smiled. She knew she could count on Linh to help her.

The two girls pulled blankets off the beds and laid them out in the middle of the floor. Tuyet picked up one of the crying babies. A care worker walked over to take the baby away from her.

Tuyet held up one hand. "*No*," she said.

Linh picked up another baby. They placed the babies on the blanket so close that they were touching. The babies stopped crying. Tuyet and Linh picked up two more babies and placed them on the blanket, so close to the others that they, too, were touching. Those babies stopped crying, as well.

One of the workers smiled in understanding. "Come," she said to the others. "Let's get these babies together so they can get some sleep."

Once the babies and toddlers were asleep, the room seemed unnaturally quiet to Tuyet. All her life, she had been surrounded by noise.

"Can I sleep beside you on your cot?" Tuyet asked Linh.

"I would like that," said Linh.

In no time, the two exhausted girls were fast asleep.

In the morning, the workers turned their efforts to Linh

and Tuyet. Each had to give up her clothing. They had a shower in a white-tiled bathroom that smelled of antiseptic. After the shower, they came out, shivering, and were wrapped in towels. The workers gave them each a pair of pants, a sweater, socks, and a small white cotton item.

"What is this?" Tuyet asked Linh, holding up the small bit of cotton.

"Underwear," said Linh. "You put it on underneath your pants."

The thought made Tuyet giggle. It seemed so unnecessary. At the orphanage, Tuyet had never worn such a thing, just the pajama-like top and drawstring bottoms. She shrugged and put on the underwear. She guessed she would have to get used to more strange Canadian customs.

Tuyet's pants and sweater fit well enough, but she couldn't get the socks to stretch over her weak foot. Linh got shoes, but none fit Tuyet, so she left her feet bare.

Over the next few days, everything settled into a routine. It reminded Tuyet of the orphanage. There were no lessons or chapel, and no one rapped Tuyet's knuckles with bamboo, but eating and sleeping and washing and playing were done to a schedule.

Was this what her life would be like from now on? Tuyet didn't mind. She had the babies to help with. She had her friend Linh beside her. No helicopters flew overhead. And there was no war.

But a few days later, just as she was getting used to the routine, everything changed. People came in—men and women who didn't speak Vietnamese. Each couple took a baby away. Would all the babies be taken away? And once they were gone, where would she and Linh go? Would they be sent to another place filled with babies?

Then, one morning, it was Linh's turn.

Tuyet watched in despair as a woman and man with kind smiles sat with Linh and talked to her with hand gestures. Linh grinned with joy. She did not use the word *no*. Linh glanced over at Tuyet and a look of concern clouded her face. She motioned to the man and woman that she would be back. Then she approached Tuyet.

"They want to be my new family," she said.

"You promised you would say no," said Tuyet. "I want you to stay here with me."

"You'll be getting a family, too," said Linh. "*No* won't work." She hugged Tuyet. "I will never forget you."

Tuyet didn't hug Linh back. She pushed her away.

"Have a good life," she said, limping over to hug one of the babies before Linh could see the tears in her eyes.

The Child Welfare Act
ADOPTION ORDER

In the   County   Court of the   County   of   Brant

HIS HONOUR JUDGE

E.O. FANJOY   Thursday   , the 15th

IN CHAMBERS   day of   January   , 19 76.

In the matter of   Thi Anh Tuyet Son

resident in the Province of Ontario and born or alleged to be born in

the   City   of   Saigon

in the   Gia Dinh   xf in   xixxbxx

xProvincexxf   South Vietnam   , on the   6th   day

of   August   , 19 66.   , as appears by the

Registration Number   65463 √   on the certificate of birth

registration issued by   South Vietnam

AND IN THE MATTER OF *The Child Welfare Act.*

Upon the Application of John Charles Morris

of the   City   of   Brantford   in the   County   of

Brant   and   Dorothy Elaine Morris   his wife, both

resident in the Province of Ontario, for an order for the adoption of the said child;

Upon Reading the certificate of the   Local Director   under the said Act
                                    (Director or local director)

and upon considering what was alleged by or on behalf of the said applicants and being satisfied

that compliance has been made with the said Act:

It is Ordered:

1. That   Thi Anh Tuyet Son   be and is hereby adopted as the

    child of   John Charles Morris   and   Dorothy Elaine Morris

2. That the name of the child shall be   Tuyet Ruth Morris
        Entered O.B. '4'
        Date 15/1/76
        Initials J.A.W.
    20-00-028 (4/73)   (Judge)

Tuyet's adoption order

Chapter Six

Tuyet's Turn

Tuyet sat at a table alone, clutching the doll she had been given on her first night at Surrey Place.

She pulled off bits from a piece of bread and put them in her mouth. She did not feel hungry. She felt overwhelmingly sad, but Tuyet chewed on the bread anyway. After all, if she no longer had a job to do, they might stop feeding her.

Linh had not been gone for more than an hour, but it felt like forever to Tuyet. The loneliness sat like a weight on her shoulders.

One of the workers said something in English to Tuyet. She looked up.

Standing beside the worker was a woman holding onto the hands of two girls. The older child had a face that looked similar to the woman's and the younger one had a lovely golden complexion. A friendly-looking man stood beside them, grinning. In his arms, he carried a toddler who was surely Vietnamese. Confused, Tuyet looked back at the woman. Her eyes were brimming with tears. The girls looked as if they could barely contain their excitement.

All at once, Tuyet understood. Each couple had chosen only one baby. And Linh was the only child chosen by the last couple. All of them had found families. But this couple already had three children. What they needed was a helper.

And they had chosen Tuyet for the job.

At first, her heart felt crushed with disappointment. Deep down, she had hoped to be treated like the other children, but when had *that* ever happened?

Tuyet pasted on a brave smile, but she was still afraid. Did they know about her weak leg and foot? Maybe they wouldn't even want her as a helper once they saw her foot. All her life, she had worked hard to prove herself useful. She would just have to prove herself once more. Better to get it over with right away.

Tuyet put her bread down and pushed herself into

a standing position. With her doll clutched in one hand, she limped to their side of the table and waited, her eyes cast down. She expected them to walk away.

But they didn't.

Tuyet felt a pair of arms around her shoulders. The woman knelt beside her and held her tight. She said something in English, but the only word Tuyet could understand was *Mom*.

Tuyet's memory flashed to the woman who had visited her in the orphanage in Saigon. Had that been her mom—the woman who stopped visiting? Was that woman no longer Tuyet's mom?

Did this woman really want to be her mom? Tuyet was thrilled at the possibility. But what if this woman changed her mind, too? Tuyet became anxious to leave, *now*, before anyone had a chance to reconsider.

The care workers didn't want Tuyet to leave barefoot. It was cold for April, and it was raining. They found her a pair of white rubber boots that were so huge they reached past her knees. It was hard enough to walk barefoot, but in these boots, it was almost impossible. Mom put Tuyet's doll into her purse and took one of Tuyet's hands. The man held the toddler on his hip with one hand. Then he took Tuyet's other hand, while the two young girls walked beside them.

On their way out of Surrey Place, one of the workers wrote something on a piece of paper and gave it to Mom. Tuyet wondered what the paper said, but once they were outside, she didn't give it another thought.

She lifted her face to the sky. It wasn't black anymore and there were no stars. Now the sky was full of billowy gray clouds, and big droplets of water splashed on her face. It was as if the sky were crying for all that Tuyet had lost. But the cool rain that splattered on her upturned face also felt soothing, as if it could wash away the past. With each step away from the building, Tuyet felt a little less anxious.

The family hadn't changed their mind yet.

The man opened the back door of a car and the two girls climbed in. Mom opened the front passenger door and motioned for Tuyet to get in. It wasn't an easy job in the big white boots. So the man lifted her up to the seat, pulled off her boots, and put them into the trunk. He didn't seem to mind the look of her weak foot and leg at all. Tuyet slid over to the middle of the front seat. The man climbed into the driver's seat and Mom sat on her other side, with the toddler on her lap. She took the doll out of her purse and gave it back to Tuyet, who held it close.

6-2 *The Morris family. From left, Lara, John, Tuyet, Beth, Dorothy, Aaron*

As they drove away, the older girl leaned forward and said to Tuyet, "My name is Beth."

Tuyet turned around to get a better look at the two girls in the back. Both looked so happy and relaxed, like they belonged. Tuyet wondered what it would feel like to belong. She just couldn't imagine it.

"My name is Lara," said the other girl. "I'm adopted, too, but Beth is homemade."

Whatever the girl said must have been funny, because the two adults chuckled.

Beth pointed to the toddler and said, "That is Aaron. He's adopted, too."

Tuyet was pretty sure she understood three things about that conversation: the older girl's name was *Beth*, the younger girl was named *Lara*, and the baby was *Aaron*.

She pointed to herself and said, "Tuyet."

Beth clapped her hands and grinned. "Pleased to meet you, Tuyet."

Lara bounced up and down. "Hello, Tuyet!"

Beth pointed to the man who sat beside Tuyet, and said, "*Cha.*"

Cha meant *Dad*.

Tuyet knew about moms. In the orphanage, many of the children would talk longingly of their moms. But a dad was a different matter. Tuyet had listened as some children talked about their dads, but they didn't seem very real. She had never actually seen one. To her, a dad was like a made-up person, a ghost.

She thought back over the last few days. So many babies and children had been chosen by couples—men and women together. She realized that each family had a man and a woman in it. So here, in this country, it seemed, dads were more than ghosts.

Out of the corner of her eye, Tuyet looked at this man, this *actual* dad. He seemed friendly.

Tuyet listened to the girls chattering away in the back. Beth seemed to be around four years old and Lara was a bit younger. Aaron couldn't be more than two.

Tuyet heard the crinkle of paper from the back seat. She turned to look. Beth had opened up a small package of crackers. She gave one to Tuyet and one to Lara. Tuyet looked at the cracker. She was not in the habit of saying no to food. Who knew when she would have a chance to eat again? But she was so nervous that her stomach was doing flip-flops. She wasn't sure she would be able to eat.

Beth popped her own cracker, whole, into her mouth and chewed. Lara took nibbling bites. Tuyet didn't want to say no. Even though Linh had told her that *no* was the magic word in English, she was afraid to use it now. Maybe they would return her to Surrey Place if she didn't like the food they gave her.

She took a bite of the cracker, then another.

Soon it was gone.

Beth handed her a second cracker and she ate that one, too. But then Beth gave her another, and another. Tuyet didn't want any more crackers, but she was afraid to refuse them. She did not want the family to be angry with her.

Tuyet's stomach lurched with queasiness. She wasn't sure if it was from so many crackers, the car ride, or the excitement of being with this family. She looked behind at Beth and was thankful to see that the package of crackers was empty.

Tuyet looked out the front window and watched trees and buildings speed by, but that didn't help her stomach. She could feel the crackers rising in her throat. What should she do? She couldn't very well throw up in this fancy car! She would be taken back to Surrey Place for sure.

Tuyet swallowed and tried to breathe slowly. She

put both hands over her mouth. She tried to swallow down a gag.

They traveled in silence for a while, and Tuyet concentrated on not being sick. The car turned off the busy road and onto smaller winding ones. Tuyet looked out the window and saw houses, each one a different color. Some houses were made of wood and others were stone or brick. Flowers and sometimes big trees grew in front of them. Each house sat on a smooth carpet of green—it reminded Tuyet of rice paddies. The sight calmed her. It was good to know that one of her favorite foods grew in Canada.

For a moment, she forgot about her upset stomach.

Dad pulled into the driveway of a gray brick house with cheerful red trim. Flowers grew up through rocks, and a rice paddy sat in front.

"We're home!" cried the girls in the back. As soon as the car stopped, Lara opened her door and hopped out. Beth was close behind.

Now that the car was no longer moving, Tuyet hoped that her stomach would settle down.

Mom opened up the passenger door and got out with Aaron in her arms. Dad opened up his door and went to the trunk to bring Tuyet her boots. He set them on the driveway in front of her.

Just as she was sliding her feet into the boots, Tuyet felt her stomach roiling once again. She put her hands over her face, but this time she couldn't stop. Vomit shot out of her mouth and all over her clothing, doll, and boots. She stumbled forward, anxious to keep the vomit away from the car.

To her horror, the last of the vomit came out over Dad's shoes.

Chapter Seven

Home

Viet orphan joins city family

By MARY-ANNE HLADISH
Expositor Staff Writer

th? Morrises already have two
adopted children of mixed racial
origin.

the Sunday get-together it was
amazing to observe how all the
children communicated with

wait until September to give
Tuyet time to learn English.

7-1   *Headline from the* Brantford Expositor, *April 23, 1975*

Tuyet was afraid. She held her breath. What would this man do to her now?

Would he return her to Surrey Place?

His voice didn't sound angry. She couldn't understand the words, but she could tell he was not upset. Tuyet looked up. He was smiling. She had just ruined his shoes and he was smiling! He didn't seem to mind at all.

Lara tugged on Tuyet's hand and grinned. "Don't

worry," she said. "I throw up sometimes, too."

"Come on," Beth said excitedly. "I want to show you around."

"She needs a bath first," said Mom.

Tuyet looked at all the moving lips and tried to understand. It was impossible to know what the words meant, but Tuyet could tell that nobody was angry with her.

Dad picked Tuyet up, ignoring the mess, and carried her across the rice paddy. Tuyet looked down. There was no water and the blades were not long enough. It wasn't a rice paddy at all. Instead, it was some sort of plant that grew straight and close together. It made her sad to think that no rice would grow in front of the house she lived in. But she was curious about this new plant and yearned to touch it. Why were all the blades the same length?

When they got into the house, Tuyet breathed in the fresh smell of lemongrass, which made her think of a time before the orphanage. The inside was open and cheerful, with white walls and colorful furniture and pictures. The floor was covered with a shaggy gold carpet. It felt homier than the stark white of Surrey Place, with its smell of bleach.

Dad set Tuyet down in the bathroom and left. Mom

came in and filled the tub with water. She squirted in some liquid from a bottle, and sweet-smelling bubbles immediately appeared. Tuyet frowned in confusion. She had always bathed herself with a basin of water and a rag. At Surrey Place, she showered to keep clean. Why did they think she needed this huge amount of water?

Mom helped her slip out of her dirty clothing, and then she motioned for Tuyet to get into the tub.

Tuyet reached into the tub and scooped up a handful of the soapy water to show Mom how she could clean herself without getting into the tub. Mom shook her head. She lifted Tuyet up and placed her in the water.

At first, Tuyet was frightened, but the warm bubbly water felt wonderful, and it soothed her weak foot. She began to relax.

Mom helped her wash thoroughly, from the tips of her fingers to the bottoms of her toes. When Tuyet thought she was finished, Mom filled a bowl with the sudsy water. She held it over her own head to demonstrate what she was going to do. Tuyet nodded. She tilted her head back and felt the warm water spill all over her scalp and down her shoulders. Mom squirted out another liquid into the palm of her hand and worked it into Tuyet's scalp. The soap had a light, clean, and fresh scent.

Beth came in with a hand mirror. When Tuyet saw what she looked like with a mound of white foamy bubbles on her head, she laughed out loud. Mom rinsed it all out with fresh water from the tap and then she helped Tuyet out of the tub.

Tuyet had no clothing except for the dirty outfit from Surrey Place, so Mom wrapped her in a towel. Beth brought in some of her clothing for Tuyet to try on, but Tuyet was much taller and thinner than Beth. Nothing fit.

Mom got one of her own t-shirts and pulled it over Tuyet's head. The end of the shirt came down below Tuyet's knees. Mom knotted it so that it fit better.

"We're going to have to take you shopping," she said.

Beth loaned her a pair of underwear. Dad found some warm woolen socks that were stretchy enough to fit over Tuyet's weak foot without hurting it.

Lara stood in the doorway and chatted away, smiling. It didn't seem to matter that Tuyet had no idea what she said. Once Tuyet was dressed, Lara clasped one hand and Beth took the other. The three girls walked downstairs to the kitchen.

Mom sat Tuyet down at the table, put a piece of cloth

on her lap, and set a bowl in front of her. It was filled with green leaves with a dollop of thick, dark orange liquid in the middle. After being sick over the crackers, Tuyet wasn't hungry. But that didn't matter—nothing put in front of her would ever go to waste.

Lara and Beth sat on either side of Tuyet, and Mom gave them each a bowl and cloth, as well. Dad put Aaron in a high chair and gave him a bowl of the greens but without the orange liquid on it. Dad was preparing other food over at the stove and Mom went over to help him.

Tuyet was about to pick up one of the green leaves with her fingers. But she stopped and peeked over at Lara and Beth, who had picked up a pronged instrument that did not look like chopsticks.

"It's a fork," said Beth, holding hers up to Tuyet. "Here's how to use it." She speared a few of the orange-doused leaves with the fork and shoved them into her mouth.

"Mmmm," said Beth. "I love Catalina dressing."

Lara held her fork with her fist and concentrated on her bowl. Aaron had another method. He grabbed the leaves one at a time with his fingertips and stuffed them in his mouth.

Tuyet picked up her fork and held it with her fist. She tried to push the sharp prongs into the leaves but it felt too awkward. She set the instrument down and held the bowl to her mouth. She opened her mouth wide and, with her fingers, guided a few leaves coated with the Catalina dressing on her tongue.

Tuyet's mouth was filled with the vilest taste she had ever experienced. The Catalina dressing had a horrible slimy texture, and it was oddly sweet and sour at the same time. She could feel the remnants of the crackers rise up in her throat. But she chewed slowly and swallowed the disgusting slime down.

There was still a lot more in her bowl. She took to the chore bravely, one awful mouthful at a time. There was no way she could let this family know that she hated their food.

Mom brought a steaming container to the table and set it down. She regarded Tuyet's empty salad bowl and the expression on the girl's face.

"Don't eat it if you don't like it," said Mom.

Dad and Mom brought more covered containers and bigger flat dishes to the table. Then Mom opened the covered containers and filled each plate with some of the contents. She set one of the plates in front of Tuyet, who examined it. A piece of something pale brown, some yellow roundish things, and a scoop of white rice.

Tuyet's heart leapt at the sight of the rice. Holding the plate up, she shoveled the rice into her mouth with her fingers. She ate every last grain. The rice appeared to settle her stomach, so Tuyet picked up one of the yellow round things. It was slightly sweet and Tuyet liked the taste, but she didn't think she'd be able to eat them all. She picked up the brown piece of food—it looked like fish—and took a bite. It had a similar texture to the fish served at the orphanage, but it was tougher and bland. In the airplane, all the children were fed a broth with rice in it; sometimes there were chunks in it like this. One of the workers who spoke Vietnamese had told Tuyet it was called *chicken*. Tuyet took another bite.

All of a sudden, her stomach started churning. The last thing she wanted to do was to throw up again! While the others concentrated on their dinner, Tuyet took the piece of chicken and hid it in her sock.

Lara pointed at the yellow round things still on Tuyet's plate. "Corn," said Lara. "Mmmm."

Tuyet looked at the corn on her plate. Lara was right.

It did taste good, but she was too full. She scooped up a handful of kernels and dropped them into her sock.

"My, you're a good eater," said Mom when she saw Tuyet's empty plate.

Once the children were finished, Dad took them back upstairs to the bathroom. He handed Tuyet a small pink stick with bristles on one end. She examined the stick carefully, not knowing what to do with it. Beth and Lara applied a smear of white paste onto their brushes from a tube and wet them with cold water from the sink. Beth looked into the bathroom mirror and bared her teeth. Lara giggled. Beth put the bristled end of the brush into her mouth and began to wash her teeth with it.

Tuyet understood. At the orphanage, they would use a bit of salt on a finger and clean their teeth with that. Tuyet picked up the tube and squeezed some paste on her brush. But when she put the brush in her mouth, her eyes widened in surprise. The paste did not taste at all like salt; it was an explosion of flavor. As she brushed, her mouth filled up with peppermint foam. She would have swallowed it down, but Beth and Lara spit the minty foam out into the sink and rinsed their brushes with water. Tuyet did the same.

There was so much to learn!

"Come see your bedroom," said the girls in unison, each tugging at one of her hands.

Tuyet let Beth and Lara pull her to a door across the hallway. Mom and Dad were close behind with Aaron.

Lara pushed open the door. "For you."

Tuyet stepped in. Along the wall sat a waist-height sleeping area covered with pink, soft material and topped with a puffy rectangle decorated with flowers. Her doll, freshly cleaned, was propped up on the bed. Handled compartments were tucked into a tall wooden box that stood against another wall.

The elevated sleeping area was big enough for all the children, thought Tuyet. She looked down at the floor. A nice soft rug.

Tuyet stood frozen in the doorway. She didn't know what was expected of her. Mom pointed to the room and then she pointed to Tuyet. She nodded and smiled.

Tuyet understood now. This was the place where she would sleep. But why were they all standing around and smiling at her?

Mom walked into the room, picked up the doll, and put it into Tuyet's hand. Then she pulled down the fabric on the elevated sleeping area and pretended to get in under the fabric. She motioned for Tuyet to get in.

"This is your very own bed," said Mom. Then she pointed to Tuyet's feet.

It was time to take off her socks.

Slowly Tuyet pulled down her socks and slipped them off her feet. Mom, using hand gestures, indicated that her socks should be put in a small basket in the corner. Tuyet obeyed, carefully lowering each sock into the basket.

Nobody saw the hidden food.

Relieved, Tuyet climbed up into bed and hugged her doll tight. She marveled at the softness of the mattress and the fluffiness of the pillow. She was used to sleeping flat on the floor. She put her head down on the pillow. Mom pulled the material up over Tuyet's shoulders and tucked it in around her.

Mom bent down and kissed Tuyet on the cheek. Tuyet thrilled at the touch. Dad, holding Aaron, leaned over and kissed her, too.

"Good night, dear Tuyet," he said.

Aaron patted her cheek with his chubby hand. And Lara kissed her on the forehead.

Mom lifted Beth up to the bed so that her face hovered over Tuyet's.

"Good night, sister," she said, and gave Tuyet a smacking wet kiss right on the lips.

Tuyet smiled. She loved all the contact with these new people. She hoped they liked her. Maybe they wouldn't send her back to Surrey Place after all.

But then they left the room.

Mom clicked off the light and closed the door.

Tuyet was plunged into darkness.

Chapter Eight
The Darkness

8-1   *Tuyet's passport photographs*

Tuyet waited for the door to open again and for the other
children to join her. She waited and waited and waited.
The door stayed closed. She was alone in the dark.

Tuyet clung to her doll and closed her eyes. But sleep
wouldn't come. The bed was too big for just one person.
As she pulled the soft covers up to her face, Tuyet tried
not to think of all the times when she had been left on
her own. That other mother, who stopped visiting. The

white van that took her away from the special boy. Linh, who had left her for that family. They all came back to Tuyet, like a nightmare she was helpless to stop. Would she always be alone?

Would she ever be important to a family that already had two girls and a boy?

Tuyet set her doll down. Swinging her legs over the side of the bed, she slipped out and limped over to the tall wooden box against the wall. She caressed the top and was comforted by its smooth coolness. If the box was in her room, did that mean the family had given it to her? What a huge possession. Her hand brushed down the front of the box and her fingertips landed on the first handle. She pulled. A drawer slid out, bigger than the boxes that had carried the babies to Canada. Tuyet pushed herself up as tall as she could and felt inside. Nothing there.

She limped to the clothing hamper, took out her socks, and carried them back to the top drawer. Holding the socks by the toes, she gave them a shake. Kernels of corn and the piece of chicken fell out. When her socks were empty, she pushed the food with her fingertips into the back corners of the drawer.

If they forgot to feed her, at least she would have something to eat.

Tuyet stepped to the window and drew back the curtains. The stars filled the dark sky—so many that she could not count them. So bright and sparkling. So beautiful. It was the best thing about her new country, seeing the stars, knowing they weren't bombs or helicopters and couldn't hurt her.

She left the curtains open and climbed back into bed. She hugged her doll and thought of Surrey Place, where she, Linh, and the babies had slept so close to one other.

Tuyet wondered if the others slept by themselves. She walked to her door and opened it a crack. She could hear rhythmic breathing coming from one of the rooms and a gentle snore from another. She pulled the door open wider—

Squeak!

Tuyet started. She held her breath. Had she woken anyone?

But the rhythmic breathing continued.

If she limped down the hallway, she was sure to make noise. She had only one choice. Tucking her doll into the neck of her shirt, she got down onto the floor and dragged herself silently along the hallway until she reached the first door. She pulled herself up with care and turned the doorknob slowly. Terrified of another *squeak*, she held her breath and pushed the door open just far enough to peek inside.

The room was similar to hers, but this one had a bed on either side. Between the beds was a window, the curtain opened slightly. On the floor sat a small rug, just like in her room. In one bed, Tuyet could make out the form of Beth snuggled up under the covers, her long hair splayed out over the pillow. In the other was Lara, deep in sleep on her back, her arms flung above her head.

Tuyet longed to sleep in this room with the two girls. Their closeness would comfort her. The sound of their breathing would lull her nightmares away. She softly closed the door and crawled to the next bedroom. This one was smaller. Tuyet could see the barred sides of Aaron's crib. He slept, curled in a ball, in one corner of the crib.

The low snoring noise got a little louder as Tuyet made her way to the end of the hall. At the convent, one of the older nuns snored, so the sound did not frighten Tuyet. If anything, she found it a comfort. She gingerly pushed open the door and poked her head in. Mom and Dad were sound asleep in their bed.

Tuyet closed the door as gently as she could and headed back along the hall. But instead of passing Beth and Lara's room, she stopped for a moment and leaned against the door. How she longed to go into that room and sleep on the rug between them.

It was so frightening to think of sleeping alone. But she didn't want to disappoint this family. She had to make herself agreeable so they would never think of sending her back.

Tuyet returned to her own room.

She knew she would never sleep if she got back into the soft bed, so she hugged her doll and curled up on the rug. She'd wake up early and get into the bed.

No one would know the difference.

Chapter Nine

Dad

The first bits of daylight warmed Tuyet's face. In her dreams, she was still in the orphanage, sleeping on the wood slat floor. She opened her eyes. She was on a rug on the floor. She sat up and felt her cheek. It was rippled with the impression of a soft rug instead of wooden slats.

It all came back to her in a rush. She was alone, but this room, the too-soft bed, the chest of drawers where she'd hidden extra food—they were all her very own. And the stars...

She limped to the window. The morning sky was a crisp bright blue with tufted clouds, and the ground was carpeted in green. There were objects on the green, but she didn't quite know what they were.

The doorknob was turning! Tuyet grabbed her doll

and jumped into the bed just as the door squeaked open. Mom walked in, smiling, carrying Tuyet's freshly laundered pants and her sweater from Surrey Place. But as soon as Mom saw Tuyet's face, her smile disappeared.

"What happened to your cheek?"

Mom placed the clothing on the dresser and sat down on the bed. She touched the spot on Tuyet's cheek where the rug had made its mark. Tuyet was scared. Would she be punished for sleeping on the floor? The woman didn't seem angry, but she wasn't happy either.

All at once, Mom wrapped her arms around Tuyet, drawing her in close. It felt so good to be held. It almost felt like being safe.

Just then, Lara and Beth tumbled into the room, hair awry, still in their pajamas.

"Good morning, Tuyet," said Lara.

"Morning, sister," said Beth. "I heard you outside our room last night."

Tuyet didn't know what the girls were saying, but she could see right away that Beth's words had caught Mom's attention.

"Tuyet was in the hallway last night?" Mom asked.

"She was outside our door for a long time," said

Beth. "I don't think she likes sleeping alone."

Mom patted the bed. "Let's all give Tuyet a hug."

The girls climbed up onto the bed. Soon they were all over Tuyet, hugging and tickling until they all dissolved in a fit of giggles.

Mom looked at her wristwatch. "Girls," she said, "it's time to get dressed. We're going to be late for church."

Beth grabbed Lara's hand and the two girls ran to their own bedroom.

Mom pointed to the freshly laundered clothing that she had set on top of the dresser and hurried out.

Tuyet put on her Surrey Place clothes and went down the hallway to the bathroom. Lara and Beth were dressed and at the sink, brushing their teeth. Mom was kneeling beside the tub, bathing Aaron.

Tuyet couldn't help Beth and Lara brush their teeth, but she was determined to show Mom that she could be a good worker. Tuyet knelt beside Mom at the side of the tub and tried to edge her out of the way. She grabbed the face cloth from Mom's hand.

Mom took the face cloth back. "You are my daughter," she said. "Not my helper."

Tuyet was confused. Why was she here if not to

help with the children?

Mom pointed to Beth and Lara and made motions like brushing her teeth. Tuyet stood up and stepped over to the sink. At least she could understand Mom some of the time.

Tuyet followed Beth and Lara to the kitchen, where Dad was setting out bowls, spoons, milk, and a mysterious box. Tuyet sat in a chair between the two younger girls. Beth poured what looked like small pebbles from the box into her bowl, and passed the box to Tuyet, who copied her then handed the box to Lara. Lara poured milk all over the pebbles, so Tuyet did the same.

"Cheerios," said Lara, picking up her spoon and pointing it at the box.

Tuyet examined her spoon. It looked like a more practical tool than the pronged instrument from the evening before. She dipped the spoon into her bowl, filled it, and tasted the pebbles. They were crunchy and sweet—much better than Catalina dressing!

The spoon was slowing her down, so Tuyet picked up her bowl and slurped down her breakfast. She gave a loud burp to show that she appreciated the good food. Dad looked over in surprise, but he didn't comment.

Tuyet had just finished her breakfast when Mom arrived, wearing a fancy outfit and carrying Aaron on her hip. She didn't sit down for breakfast.

"We're going to be late for church," she said.

Beth and Lara quickly finished their Cheerios and got up from the table, taking their bowls and spoons with them and depositing them in the kitchen sink.

Tuyet stood up to follow the girls, but Mom put up her hand and said, "No. We need to buy you shoes on Monday. You can come to church with us next week."

Tuyet didn't understand.

Mom pointed to her own feet, and then to Tuyet's. "No shoes," she said.

Tuyet had no shoes. She understood that much.

Mom kissed Dad on the cheek. Then she carried Aaron out the door. Beth and Lara followed.

Tuyet hobbled to the front door as quickly as she could. She reached the handle and was almost outside when Dad put his hand on her shoulder.

"No," he said.

Tuyet looked up at him in confusion. He didn't seem angry. The two of them stood together in the doorway and watched Mom drive off with the children.

Tuyet and Dad were left by themselves.

So it *was* too good to be true. This woman didn't want to be her mom after all. Beth, Lara, and Aaron weren't going to be her family. She wasn't going back to Surrey Place. Instead, they were going someplace else and she was staying here. But why had they left Dad behind, as well?

Maybe Tuyet had misunderstood. Maybe Dad wasn't a part of the family. Maybe dads didn't really exist in this country, either.

Tuyet felt like sitting down on the floor and bursting into tears, but what would this man do to her if she cried? Feeling like her feet were made of heavy stones, she headed slowly back to the kitchen. Two bowls and spoons were left on the table. She picked them up and carried them to the sink.

Dad filled the sink with soapy water. This was something she could do. She placed her hands on Dad's hip and pushed, trying to get him to move away from the sink. He looked down at her and smiled, but he didn't move over.

Dad washed all the dishes, rinsed them, and put them on the drying rack. When he was finished, he took two towels out of the drawer and handed her one. He dried one of the bowls and set it in the cupboard. She dried one bowl and handed it to him.

"Thank you," he said.

But soon they were done. How could she prove herself useful now?

Tuyet stood warily as Dad went to the closet. He brought out the white rubber boots. Her heart sank. So she was going back to Surrey Place, after all. But how would they get there without the car? Tuyet hoped that she wouldn't have to walk. It seemed a long distance.

Dad motioned for her to join him by the big window, and held her steady as she stepped into the tall boots. He slipped his own feet into a pair of shoes and pushed on the giant window.

It slid open! It wasn't a window, but a glass door.

Dad took Tuyet's hand and the two of them stepped outside onto a wooden porch. The air was cooler than the day before and a shiver ran through Tuyet. Dad went back inside and came out with a sweater. He popped it over her head and she slipped her arms into the sleeves, which were so long, they went down practically to her knees. Dad rolled the sleeves up until her hands peeked out. The sweater was cozy and warm. She looked up at Dad and smiled.

He stepped down onto the green carpet and Tuyet followed him. She wanted to touch the green stems, but her boots were so tall that it was hard to crouch down. Dad sat right down on the green and patted the spot beside him. Tuyet sat, her giant boots splayed out in front of her. She placed her palm down on the green and felt its cold dampness.

"*Grass*," said Dad. He pulled out one blade and handed it to her.

Tuyet examined it carefully. It was a perfect, tiny knife of green.

Dad ran his hand through the grass as if he were looking for something.

"There's one," he said, pulling up a broad piece of grass. He held it flat between his two thumbs and brought it to his lips. He blew, making a shrill, whistling noise.

At first Tuyet was startled by the noise, but Dad did it again, and she found the noise so absurd that she giggled. He showed her how he held the blade. Tuyet held hers between her thumbs. She brought it to her lips and blew, but it didn't work. Dad combed his fingers through the grass and found another broad blade and handed it to her.

It took her a few tries, but soon she was making as much noise as Dad. He laughed out loud and she grinned. Maybe it would be okay, after all.

Dad stood up and held out his hand to help Tuyet to her feet. He pointed to one of the objects that she had seen from her bedroom window. It was a metal framework with pairs of rope hanging down, a wooden slat between each pair of ropes.

"*Swing*," Dad said.

Tuyet stared at him in confusion. Dad sat on one of the seats. He pushed off with his feet and swung back and forth. Tuyet couldn't help but smile. It seemed like such an odd thing to do. Dad hopped off the swing, picked her up, and placed her on it, showing her where to hold the ropes so that she would be steady. She gripped the rope. It was an odd sensation, like floating in the air. Dad stood behind her and gave her a gentle push.

Tuyet smiled.

Dad pushed her a bit more. The swing rocked gently back and forth, and Tuyet felt the wind on her face. The sky and the grass sped up before her. It seemed like such a wasteful thing to do—sitting, feeling the swing go back and forth, watching the world speed up. It didn't seem to have any purpose at all. Tuyet did not feel useful sitting there.

But she could have stayed on it for hours.

It was...fun!

Tuyet was so entranced that she didn't notice her hands were starting to turn blue with the cold. But Dad saw. He put his hands on the rope and steadied the swing until it stopped. He lifted her off and held her in his arms. She clung to him and felt his warmth.

Dad carried Tuyet around the yard. He pointed at objects and told her what their English names were—*sandbox, monkey bars, back porch, fence.* It seemed there was no end to the marvels of the backyard.

"*Play,*" he said, holding one arm out wide.

They walked up the porch steps and through the sliding glass door. Dad set her back on her feet and pointed to the table. She sat on one of the chairs. Dad left the room. Within moments, he was back, carrying a worn cardboard box. He upended the contents onto the table. Wooden blocks.

Dad and Tuyet spent the rest of the morning building tall towers and knocking them down.

Tuyet heard the sound of a car pulling into the driveway.

"Mom, Aaron, Beth, and Lara are home," said Dad.

Tuyet ran to the front door. It was true! They had come back! Beth was first through the door, with Lara close behind her.

"Want to play outside?" she asked Tuyet.

Tuyet knew *play*. She knew *outside*. She nodded.

là tình yêu đẹp xinh mến chúa yêu người là
điều răn chúa anh em hãy tôn thờ những
lời ngài đã ban.

Bài ca (8)
Em viết chữ y
Em viết chữ y, em viết chữ ê, em thêm chữ u, em
lòng dạ yêu yêu cha là mẹ, yêu ông là yêu bà, yêu cô
bác gần xa em yêu là yêu.

Bài ca (9)
Đám cưới trên đường quê hương
Ồ, ồ sáng hôm nay trên quê hương tây quê hương
sinh sinh quê hương hữu tình, quê hương xinh xinh quê
hương hòa bình đường làm sao trắng xanh vàng tím
đẹp làm sao bướm bay chập chờn dân chín non réo
lên ngọn tre thân màu xo áo màu hồng ơi bà con
đến xem mùa cưới chân hồi công tay đủ hồng ra
mà xem mới thấy được một nhiên vui anh đi mới tình
tôi đi anh đi xem người ta hô cưới nhau rồi.
Ồ, ồ sáng hôm nay tôi ra tôi xem cô dâu non non
nhun nhắng mỹ mẹo cô dâu non non nhun nhắng mặt
mày, cha nhà cu cô ông về quí cha nhà ai có cô dâu
hiền cô thấy cô co con kắng quai tôi mười mầm cáo
đầy buồn ra mà xem mới thấy được một nhiệm vui
em đi mới tình tôi đi em đi xem người ta hô cưới
nhau rồi.

Bài ca (10)
Cái nhà
Cái nhà là nhà của ta ông cộ ông cha lập ra chúng
con hãy gìn giữ lấy muôn năm lấy m nước lau nhà.

Chapter Ten

Joy

That afternoon, Tuyet learned about making shapes in the sandbox with damp sand and a pail. She hung from the monkey bar with both hands while Beth and Lara tumbled around her. One day she would be strong enough to follow them, but for now, she only cared about being part of the family. She didn't speak the same language yet, but they all seemed to communicate fine. It still felt odd to be playing with children instead of standing back and watching. But it was a good feeling.

She was pushing Lara on the swing when Dad stepped outside.

"Tuyet," he said. He motioned with his hand for her to come in.

Had she done something wrong? She steadied the

swing and helped Lara down, then she trudged inside.

Her eyes took a few seconds to adjust to the light indoors. Three people sat at the kitchen table—a man, a woman, and a girl. She blinked. She had seen this man and woman before. She looked at the girl.

It couldn't possibly be. She rubbed her eyes and blinked again.

"Linh?"

10-1   *Tuyet with Linh, May 1975*

The girl jumped out of the chair so quickly that she nearly upended it. She ran to Tuyet and wrapped her arms around her.

Tuyet hugged her friend and wept and wept.

"How did you find me?" she asked when she could speak again.

"It was a care worker," said Linh. "Someone told our parents about our friendship. We live close enough to visit."

"Come on," said Tuyet. "I want you to meet Beth and Lara. And you've got to see the big outside with all the play things."

Linh stayed the entire afternoon. Tuyet was so happy that her heart felt like it would burst.

When it was time for bed, Tuyet was so filled with contentment that she thought she might be able to sleep on her own. The happy memories of the day would drive out her fears. But when she went into her bedroom, something had changed. The bed was bare.

Tuyet turned. Beth stood in the doorway, a grin on her face.

"Come on," she said. "We have another surprise for you."

Tuyet followed Beth into the girls' room. Lara sat cross-legged on her own bed. On the floor between the two beds were Tuyet's sheets, blankets, and pillow—made up like her own special bed.

"You can sleep with us as long as you want," said Lara.

That night, Tuyet slept on the floor between her two sisters, wrapped in the comforting sound of their rhythmic breathing.

In the middle of the night, she woke up and slipped out of bed. She looked out the window. They were still there, sparkling down on her.

So many stars. Too many to count.

10-2

Beth, Tuyet, Aaron, and Lara,
first day of school, 1978

Historical Note

During the course of the Vietnam War, many Vietnamese children were left orphaned. Missionary groups from all over the world came to South Vietnam and tried to help the orphans, but supplies were hard to come by and the conditions in the orphanages were awful. When South Vietnam was captured, the North Vietnamese victors wanted to close down the orphanages. Healthy South Vietnamese orphans would go to families and be brought up as loyal communists. But children with disabilities—like Tuyet—would be killed. The children of American fathers, who were considered the enemy, would also be killed.

In the spring of 1975, most American troops had already left South Vietnam. Saigon, the capital city of South Vietnam, was about to be overtaken by the Viet Cong and the North Vietnamese.

The missionaries were desperate to get out as many orphans as they could before the fall of Saigon. On April 2, 1975, fifty-seven orphans were airlifted out of Saigon on a World Airways plane. On April 4th, the first official "Operation Babylift" evacuation was to take place, but the plane crashed just after takeoff. Many orphans and care workers died.

11-1   *Colonel "Hank" Henry, Base Commander of Canadian
Forces Base Trenton, welcomes the crew of Service Flight
515 on their return from Hong Kong and Saigon*

The rescue operation described in *Last Airlift* was
the last to arrive in Canada, and there were fifty-seven
babies and children on the flight. The children arrived in
Toronto on April 13, 1975. The flight was sponsored by
the Ontario government and, unlike most of the rescue
flights before it, the children on this flight were not pre-
adopted. John and Dorothy Morris did not know that
Tuyet would become their daughter until the day before
they met her. In addition to Tuyet, John and Dorothy

were parents to Beth, their birth daughter, Aaron, from Vietnam, and Lara, from Bangladesh.

On April 14, 2006, thirty-four of the original fifty-seven orphans met in Oakville, Ontario, for a reunion. They exchanged stories and toured Surrey Place. Since that time, they have become like one big extended family. One of the original fifty-seven has died. The orphans are trying to find the other twenty-two. If you know one of these remaining orphans, please contact:

marsha@calla.com

11-2   *Master Corporal Dave Melanson, a 426 Squadron Loadmaster with the Canadian Air Force on the relief flight, with two of the children*

Further Resources for Parents and Teachers

Internet
- http://www.vietnambabylift.org/
- http://www.vietnampix.com/
(Warning: an excellent site, but some graphic images are included.)

Books
- *Beyond the Babylift: A Story of an Adoption*, by Pamela Chatterton Purdy, Abingdon Press, 1987

- *The War Cradle: Operation Babylift—The Untold Story*, by Shirley Peck-Barnes, Vintage Pressworks, 2000

Film
- *Daughter from Danang*, a co-presentation of ITVS and NAATA with *American Experience*; WGBH Boston; producer, Gail Dolgin; directors, Gail Dolgin and Vicente Franco.

Author's Note

Son Thi Anh Tuyet is now an adult, and she lives in my hometown of Brantford, Ontario. Her married name is Tuyet Yurczyszyn. She and her husband Darren bought the house Tuyet grew up in, and they have two happy, healthy children named Luke and Bria.

As part of my research, I interviewed many people. Special thanks to Thi Mai Murphy, Trent Kilner, Thanh Campbell, and Kit Spencer. Cliff Zacharias recounted his vivid memories of that fateful flight and shared his photographs. Special thanks to Dr. Georgiana Stanciu, Curator of the National Air Force Museum of Canada and also Assistant Curator, Hailey Latour. Many thanks to RCAF 426 Squadron historian Robert Fleming. Tuyet's mother, Dorothy Morris, was amazing. Her detailed recall of Tuyet's earliest days in Brantford helped me rebuild that time with accuracy. I have such admiration for Dorothy and her late husband John for their unconditional love and acceptance of not just one, but three war orphans.

In addition to the personal interviews, I read American Babylift memoirs and also watched news clips and documentaries. I pored over weeks' worth of microfilm copies of the *Brantford Expositor* and accessed *The Globe and Mail* online historical database. The *Toronto*

Star's "Pages of the Past" online database was especially helpful, as they ran a series of articles following the day-to-day progress of the last Canadian airlift, from the children's escape from Saigon until their placement with their adoptive families. Staff writer Jim Robinson's articles were particularly detailed.

When I initially approached Tuyet about this book, I was going to write it as a novel rather than non-fiction. Many of Tuyet's memories from that time were suppressed, so I was going to piece together a story of one orphan based on the experiences of many. But as I recreated these experiences from my research, an interesting thing happened. In small flashes, Tuyet began to remember more. I read every word of this story aloud to her and, as I did, she would stop and correct me. As time went on, her memories became clearer. Once, she called me the day after a marathon reading session; a random scene from television had just sparked a suppressed memory. When *Last Airlift* was complete, Tuyet was overwhelmed by the fact that it was, in fact, her own story that had been reclaimed.

Tuyet is my hero. The brave little girl whose early life was fraught with sadness and pain has grown into a remarkable woman filled with joy, generosity, and love.

Thank you, Tuyet, for sharing your story with the world.

11-3   *The author with Tuyet Yurczyszyn, spring 2011*

Marsha Forchuk Skrypuch is the author of more than a dozen historical picture books, chapter books, and juvenile and young adult novels. She has received numerous awards and nominations for her work. Her most recent novel, *Stolen Child*, has won the SCBWI Crystal Kite Award for the Americas and is an OLA Best Bet, a CLA Book of the Year nominee, a *Resource Links* Best Book, and a CCBC Our Choice starred selection. It was also nominated for three readers' choice awards: the Saskatchewan Diamond Willow, the Manitoba Young Readers' Choice, and the Ontario Golden Oak.

In 2008, in recognition of her outstanding achievement in the development of the culture of Ukraine, Marsha was awarded the Order of Princess Olha, which was bestowed upon her personally by President Victor Yushchenko. Marsha lives in Brantford, Ontario.

Tuyet would like to add her thanks.

Mom and Dad: Thank you so much for all the love. You have made me the way I am today. Also a BIG THANKS for saving my life!

Index